AF086382

What Can You Hear?

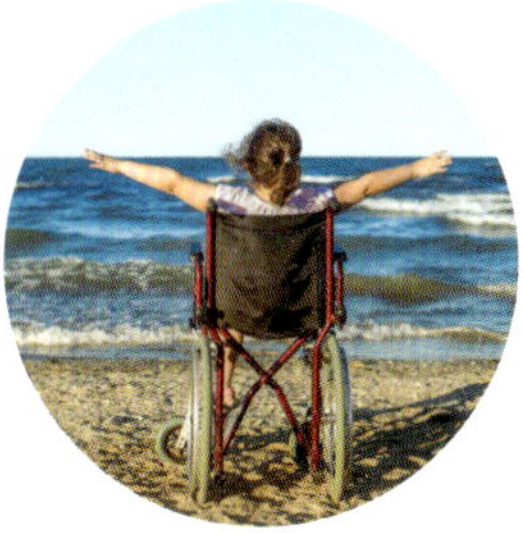

Written by
Stephen Rickard

Ransom

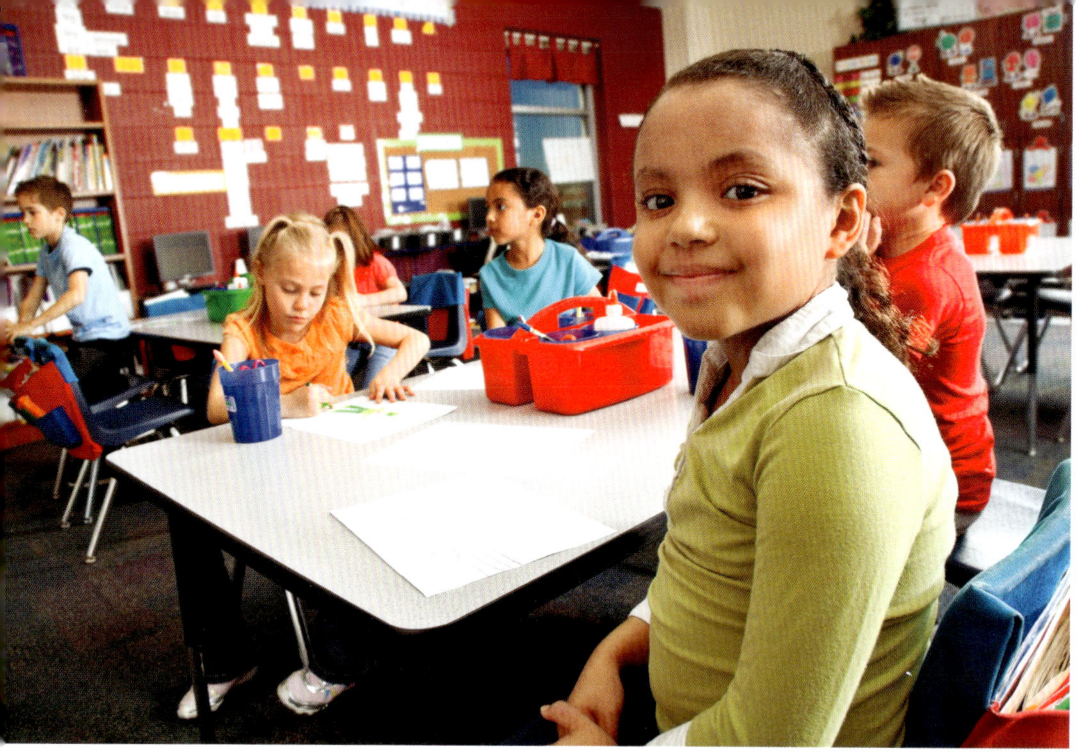

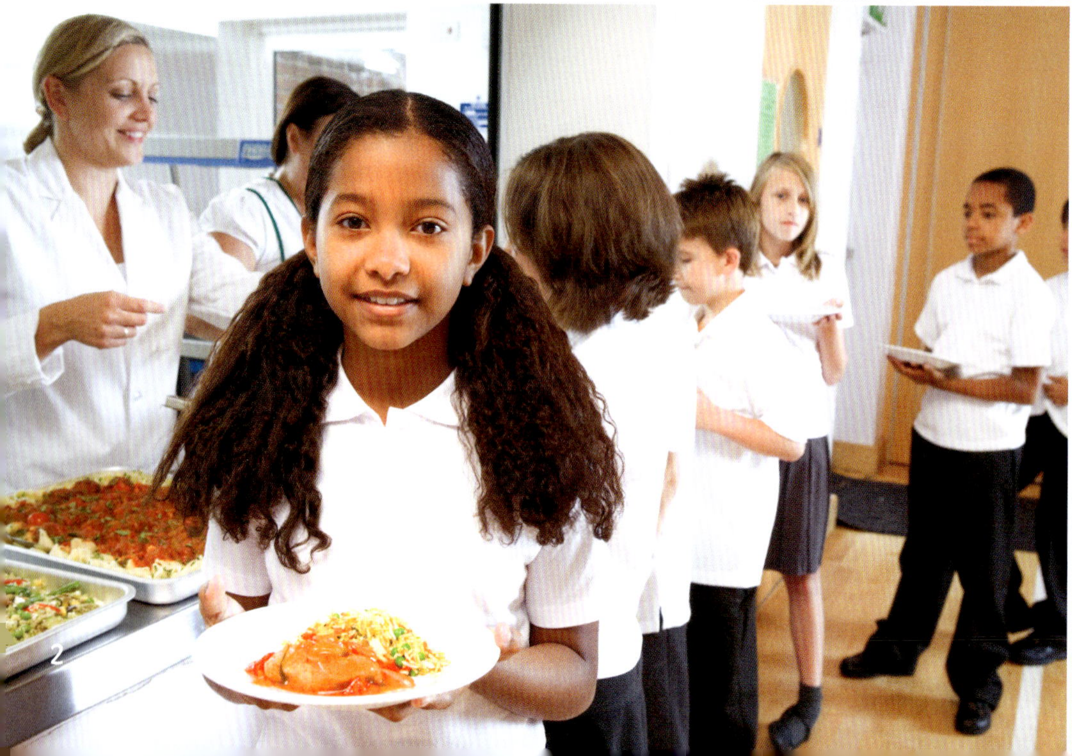

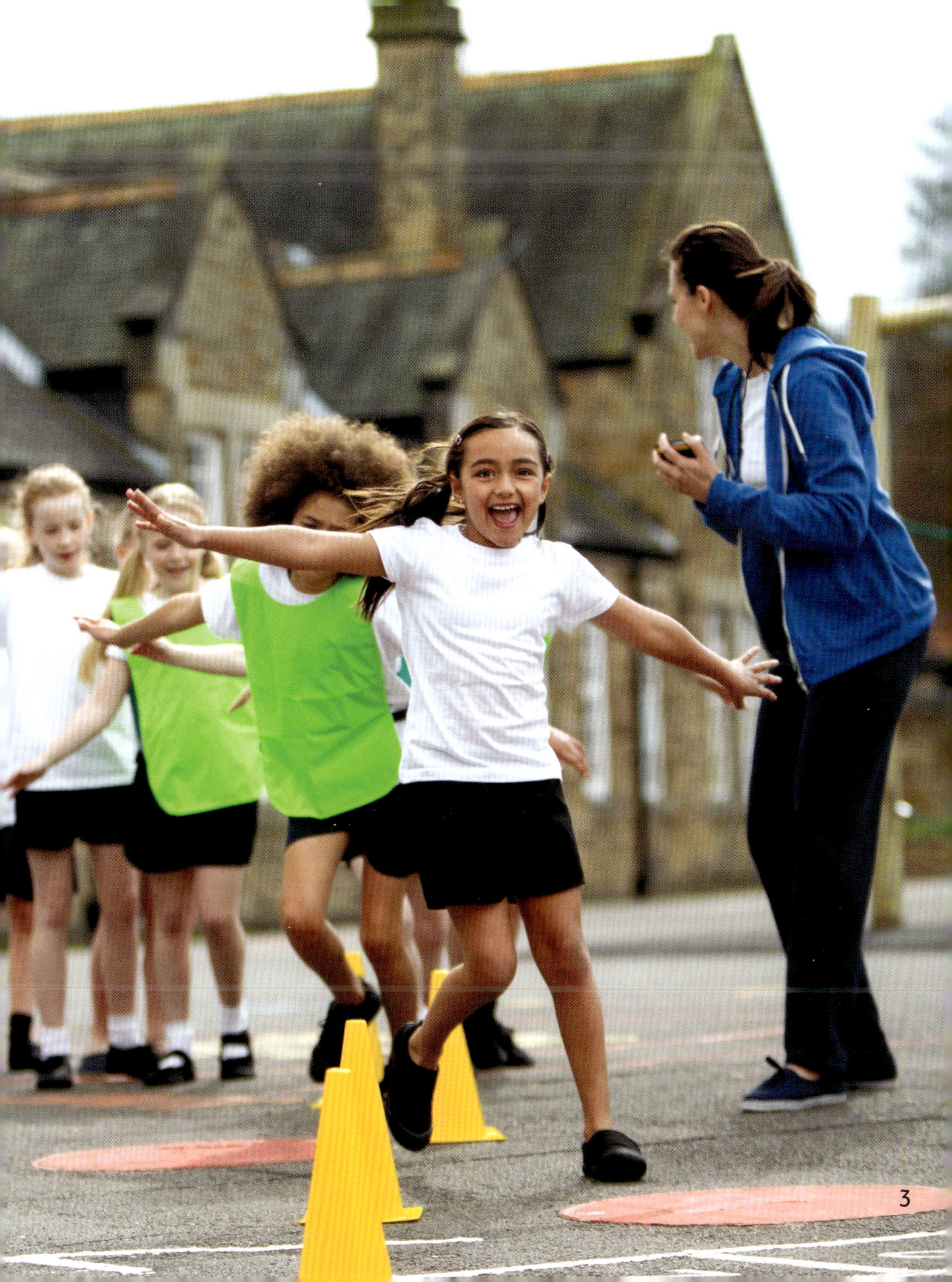

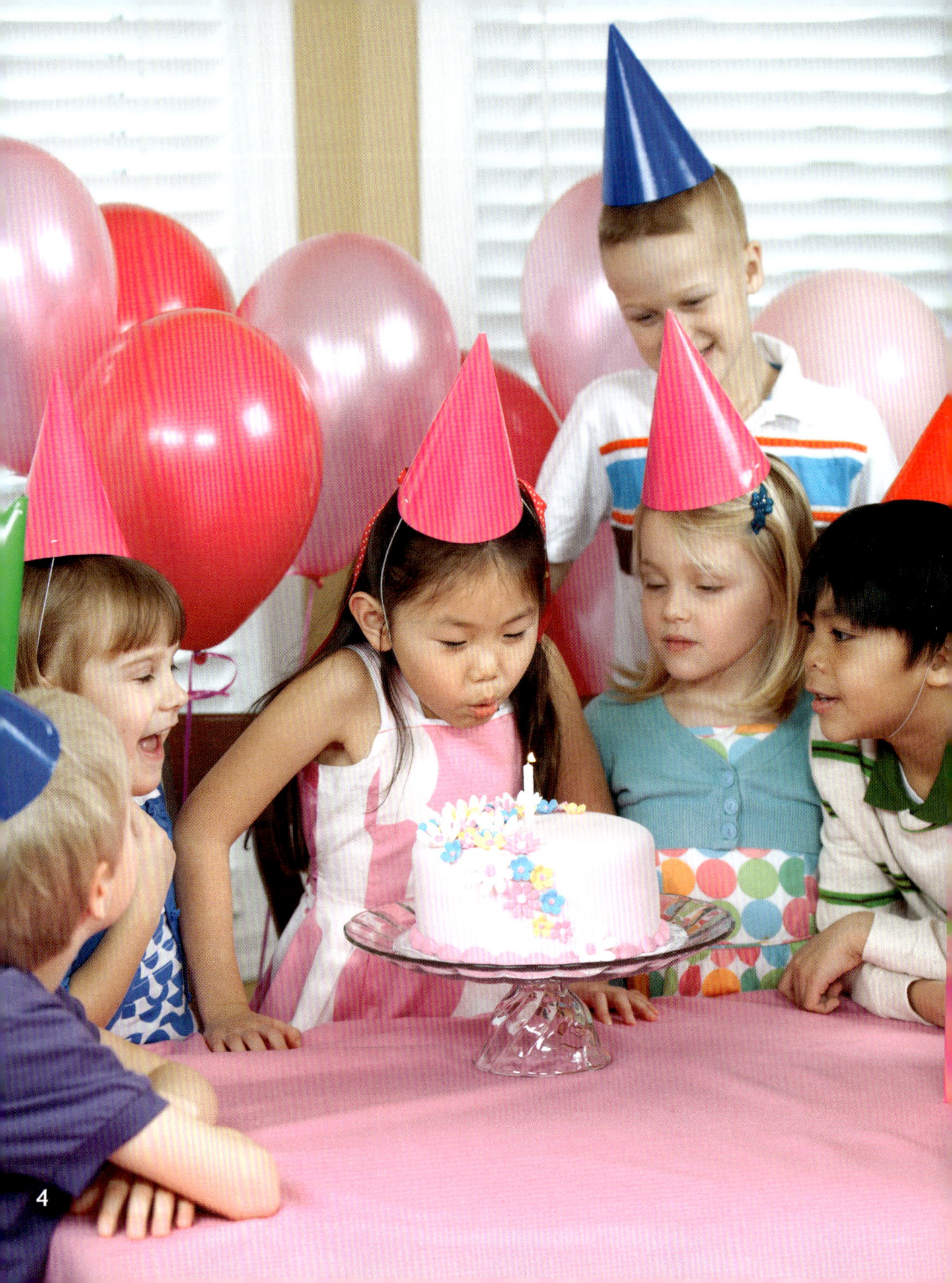

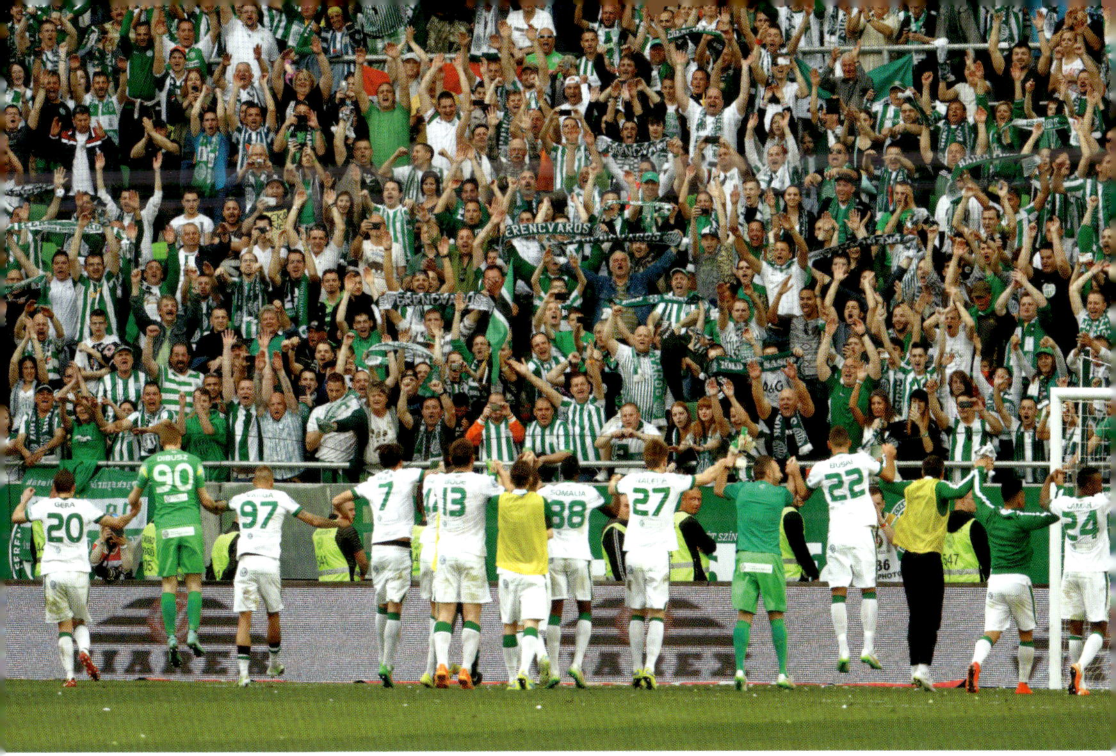

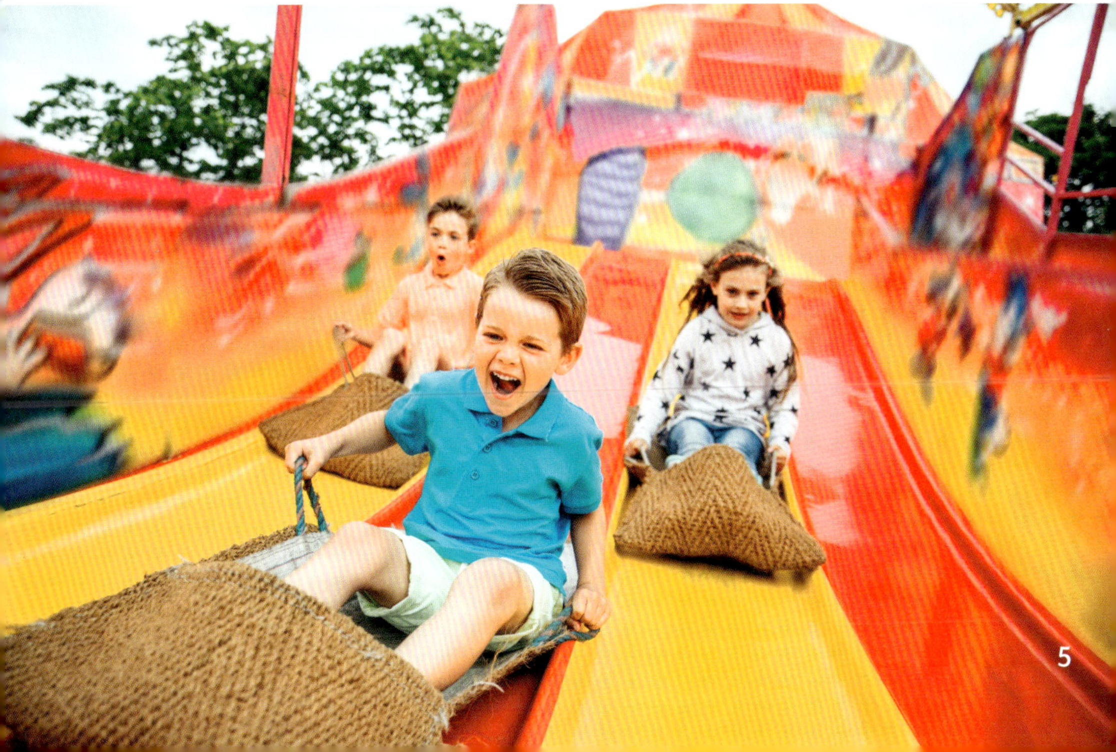

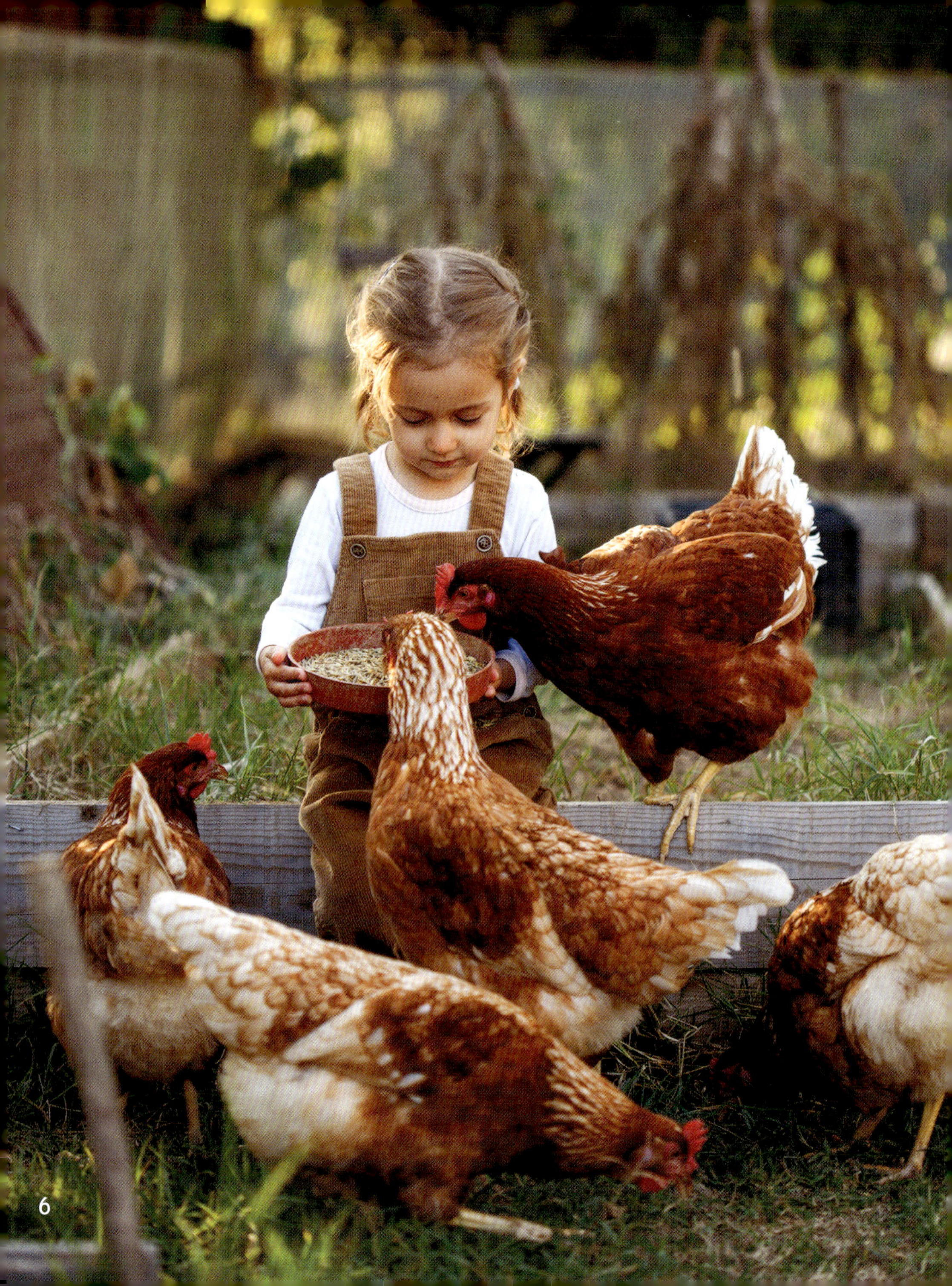

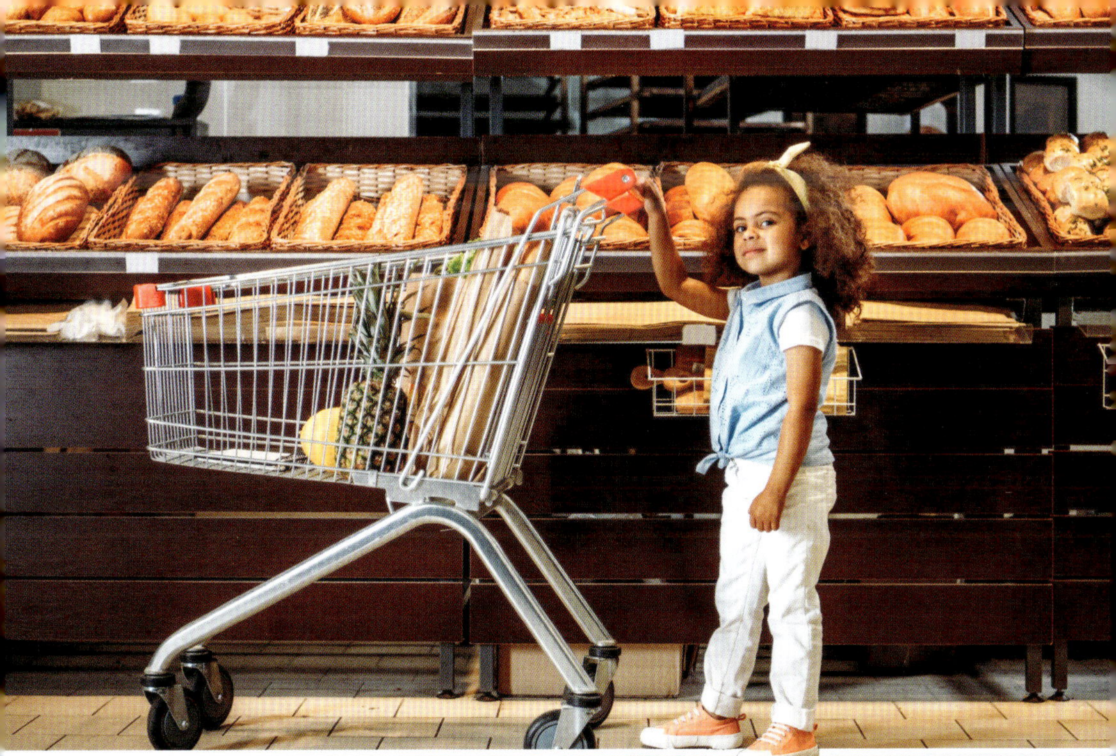

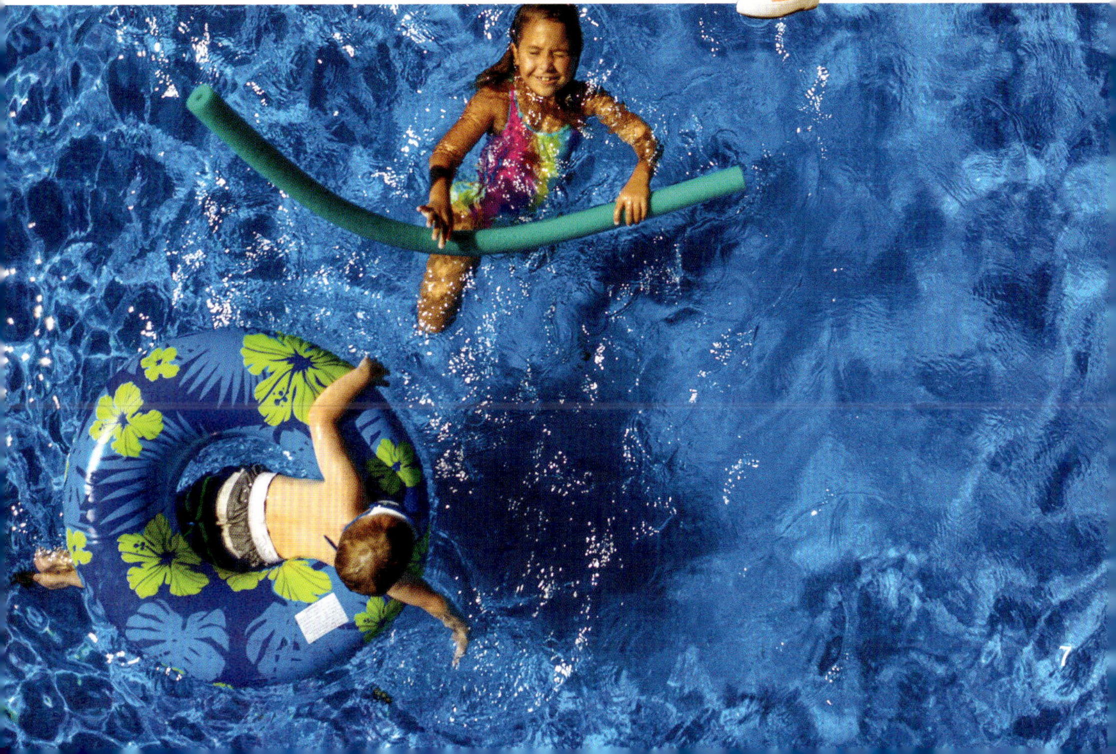

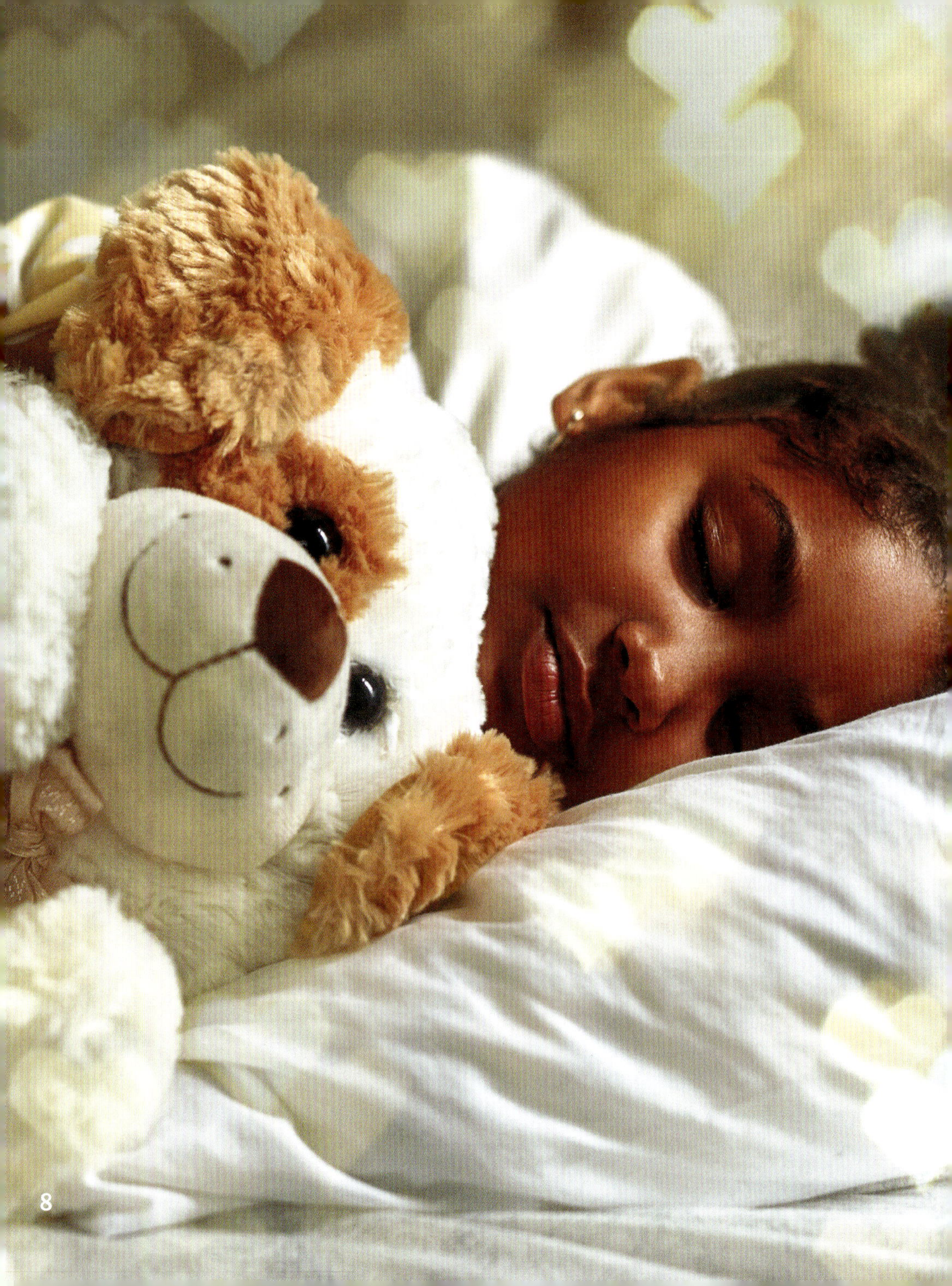